50 Breakfast from Japan Recipes

By: Kelly Johnson

Table of Contents

- Tamago Sushi
- Miso Soup with Tofu
- Japanese Pancakes (Okonomiyaki)
- Grilled Fish (Shioyaki)
- Onigiri (Rice Balls)
- Natto with Rice
- Japanese Rolled Omelette (Tamagoyaki)
- Japanese Rice Porridge (Okayu)
- Grilled Salmon with Rice
- Sweet Potato Soup
- Japanese Curry Rice (Kare Raisu)
- Tonkatsu Sandwich
- Chawanmushi (Steamed Egg Custard)
- Daifuku (Sweet Mochi)
- Rice with Pickled Plums (Umeboshi)
- Agedashi Tofu
- Japanese Toast with Butter and Soy Sauce
- Bento Box Breakfast
- Tofu Salad
- Shoku Pan (Japanese White Bread)
- Udon Noodle Soup
- Japanese-style French Toast
- Mochi with Red Bean Paste
- Japanese Hot Dog Buns
- Rice with Pickled Vegetables
- Japanese Scrambled Eggs
- Shrimp Tempura
- Miso-Marinated Fish
- Katsuobushi (Dried Bonito Flakes) on Rice
- Saba (Mackerel) with Rice
- Japanese Milk Bread (Hokkaido Milk Bread)
- Yuba (Tofu Skin) with Soy Sauce
- Sweet Red Bean Soup
- Ramen Soup with Boiled Egg
- Ebi Fry (Shrimp Fried Cutlet)
- Matcha Green Tea Pancakes

- Japanese Steamed Buns (Nikuman)
- Donburi Rice Bowls
- Mochi Ice Cream
- Tofu and Vegetable Stir-Fry
- Kake Gohan (Plain Rice with Toppings)
- Tofu and Daikon Salad
- Oyakodon (Chicken and Egg Rice Bowl)
- Okara (Soy Pulp) Patties
- Japanese-style Oatmeal
- Yakimeshi (Japanese Fried Rice)
- Japanese Hot Pot (Shabu-Shabu)
- Edamame and Rice
- Takoyaki (Octopus Balls)
- Japanese Coffee Jelly

Tamago Sushi

Ingredients:

- 2 cups sushi rice
- 1 1/4 cups water
- 2 tbsp rice vinegar
- 2 tbsp sugar
- 1/2 tsp salt
- 4 large eggs
- 1 tbsp soy sauce
- 1 tbsp mirin
- 1 tbsp vegetable oil
- Nori (seaweed) strips
- Wasabi (optional)

Instructions:

1. Rinse the sushi rice under cold water until the water runs clear. Cook the rice according to package instructions.
2. Mix the rice vinegar, sugar, and salt in a bowl until dissolved. Once the rice is cooked, transfer it to a large bowl and gently fold in the vinegar mixture. Let it cool to room temperature.
3. For the tamago (Japanese omelette), beat the eggs with soy sauce and mirin.
4. Heat a non-stick skillet over medium heat and lightly oil it. Pour a thin layer of the egg mixture into the skillet and cook until just set. Roll it to one side of the pan.
5. Pour more egg mixture into the pan and roll the cooked omelette onto the new layer. Repeat until all the egg mixture is used.
6. Slice the omelette into small pieces, and place a slice on top of a small mound of sushi rice. Wrap with a strip of nori.
7. Serve with wasabi if desired.

Miso Soup with Tofu

Ingredients:

- 4 cups dashi stock (or water with instant dashi powder)
- 3 tbsp miso paste (white or red)
- 1/2 block tofu, cut into small cubes
- 1/4 cup chopped green onions
- Wakame seaweed (optional)

Instructions:

1. In a pot, bring the dashi stock to a simmer.
2. Dissolve the miso paste into the stock by whisking it in.
3. Add the tofu cubes and simmer for 3-4 minutes.
4. Stir in the chopped green onions and wakame (if using).
5. Serve hot, garnished with additional green onions if desired.

Japanese Pancakes (Okonomiyaki)

Ingredients:

- 1 1/2 cups all-purpose flour
- 1 cup water
- 2 large eggs
- 2 cups shredded cabbage
- 1/4 cup chopped green onions
- 1/2 cup cooked pork belly or shrimp (optional)
- 1/4 cup tempura scraps (optional)
- 1 tbsp soy sauce
- 1 tbsp mirin
- 1/4 tsp baking powder
- Vegetable oil for frying
- Okonomiyaki sauce (or Worcestershire sauce)
- Kewpie mayonnaise
- Bonito flakes (optional)
- Aonori (dried seaweed flakes) (optional)

Instructions:

1. In a large bowl, whisk together flour, water, eggs, soy sauce, mirin, and baking powder.
2. Add the shredded cabbage, green onions, and optional pork belly or shrimp to the batter and mix well.
3. Heat a little oil in a large skillet over medium heat.
4. Pour the batter into the pan and cook for about 3-4 minutes per side, flipping carefully to cook the other side until golden brown.
5. Remove from the skillet and top with Okonomiyaki sauce, mayonnaise, bonito flakes, and aonori if desired.
6. Slice and serve.

Grilled Fish (Shioyaki)

Ingredients:

- 2 whole fish (mackerel, sea bream, or your choice)
- 1 tbsp salt
- Lemon wedges (optional)

Instructions:

1. Clean and gut the fish, leaving the scales intact.
2. Rub both sides of the fish with salt and let it sit for 15-30 minutes to allow the salt to draw out moisture.
3. Preheat a grill or grill pan over medium heat.
4. Grill the fish for 4-5 minutes on each side until the skin is crispy and the fish is cooked through.
5. Serve with lemon wedges if desired.

Onigiri (Rice Balls)

Ingredients:

- 2 cups cooked sushi rice
- 1 tbsp rice vinegar
- 1 tsp sugar
- 1/2 tsp salt
- Nori (seaweed) sheets
- Filling options: salted salmon, umeboshi (pickled plum), or tuna salad

Instructions:

1. Mix the rice vinegar, sugar, and salt, then fold into the warm sushi rice. Let it cool.
2. Wet your hands to prevent sticking, then scoop a small amount of rice into your palm.
3. Flatten the rice slightly and add your desired filling.
4. Mold the rice into a triangle shape, wrapping a small piece of nori around the base.
5. Serve as a snack or with a meal.

Natto with Rice

Ingredients:

- 1 pack natto (fermented soybeans)
- 1 cup steamed rice
- Soy sauce (optional)
- Mustard (optional)

Instructions:

1. Heat the natto pack according to package instructions (often served cold).
2. Place a scoop of rice into a bowl.
3. Top with the natto and mix well.
4. Add soy sauce or mustard for extra flavor, if desired.
5. Serve immediately.

Japanese Rolled Omelette (Tamagoyaki)

Ingredients:

- 4 large eggs
- 1 tbsp sugar
- 1 tbsp soy sauce
- 1 tbsp mirin
- 1/2 tsp salt
- Vegetable oil for cooking

Instructions:

1. In a bowl, beat the eggs with sugar, soy sauce, mirin, and salt.
2. Heat a rectangular or square pan over medium heat and lightly oil it.
3. Pour in a thin layer of egg mixture and cook until just set.
4. Roll the cooked egg to one side of the pan and pour in more egg mixture, lifting the rolled portion to allow the liquid to spread underneath.
5. Repeat this process until all the eggs are used.
6. Remove the rolled omelette from the pan, let it cool slightly, and slice into pieces.

Japanese Rice Porridge (Okayu)

Ingredients:

- 1/2 cup short-grain rice
- 4 cups water or dashi
- 1/4 tsp salt
- Pickled plums or sesame seeds (optional topping)

Instructions:

1. Rinse the rice until the water runs clear.
2. In a pot, combine the rice, water (or dashi), and salt.
3. Bring to a boil, then lower the heat and simmer for 30-40 minutes, stirring occasionally, until the rice breaks down and the porridge thickens.
4. Serve with pickled plums or sesame seeds on top if desired.

Grilled Salmon with Rice

Ingredients:

- 2 salmon fillets
- 1 tbsp soy sauce
- 1 tbsp mirin
- 1 tsp honey
- 2 cups cooked rice
- 1/4 cup chopped green onions (optional)

Instructions:

1. Preheat the grill or broiler to medium heat.
2. In a small bowl, mix the soy sauce, mirin, and honey.
3. Brush the salmon fillets with the marinade and let them sit for 10-15 minutes.
4. Grill the salmon for 4-5 minutes on each side until cooked through and golden.
5. Serve the salmon on top of the rice, garnished with green onions.

Sweet Potato Soup

Ingredients:

- 2 medium sweet potatoes, peeled and chopped
- 1 onion, chopped
- 1 carrot, chopped
- 1 garlic clove, minced
- 4 cups vegetable broth
- 1/2 tsp ground ginger
- 1/4 tsp ground cinnamon
- Salt and pepper to taste
- 1 tbsp olive oil

Instructions:

1. Heat olive oil in a large pot over medium heat.
2. Add onion, carrot, and garlic, and sauté for 5-7 minutes until softened.
3. Add the sweet potatoes, vegetable broth, ginger, cinnamon, salt, and pepper.
4. Bring to a boil, then reduce heat and simmer for 20-25 minutes, or until the sweet potatoes are tender.
5. Puree the soup using an immersion blender or in batches in a blender until smooth.
6. Serve hot, garnished with a dollop of cream or parsley if desired.

Japanese Curry Rice (Kare Raisu)

Ingredients:

- 1 lb chicken, pork, or beef (cut into bite-sized pieces)
- 1 large onion, chopped
- 2 carrots, peeled and chopped
- 2 potatoes, peeled and chopped
- 1/4 cup vegetable oil
- 4 cups water
- 1 package Japanese curry roux (store-bought or homemade)
- 2 cups cooked Japanese short-grain rice
- Optional: Chopped green onions or pickles for garnish

Instructions:

1. In a large pot, heat vegetable oil over medium heat. Add the onion and sauté until translucent, about 5 minutes.
2. Add the chicken, pork, or beef and cook until browned.
3. Add the carrots and potatoes to the pot, then pour in the water. Bring it to a boil, then lower the heat and simmer for about 20-25 minutes, or until the vegetables are tender.
4. Break the curry roux into chunks and add it to the pot, stirring to dissolve. Let it simmer for an additional 10-15 minutes until the curry thickens.
5. Serve the curry over a bowl of freshly cooked rice, garnished with green onions or pickles if desired.

Tonkatsu Sandwich

Ingredients:

- 2 pieces of tonkatsu (breaded and fried pork cutlets)
- 4 slices of soft white bread (shoku pan)
- 1 tbsp tonkatsu sauce
- 1 tbsp mayonnaise
- Shredded cabbage (optional)

Instructions:

1. Toast the bread slices lightly.
2. Spread tonkatsu sauce on one side of each slice of bread.
3. Place a piece of tonkatsu on one slice of bread.
4. Add a small amount of mayonnaise and top with shredded cabbage if desired.
5. Place the second slice of bread on top, sauce side down. Cut the sandwich in half and serve.

Chawanmushi (Steamed Egg Custard)

Ingredients:

- 3 large eggs
- 2 cups dashi stock
- 1 tbsp soy sauce
- 1 tbsp mirin
- 1/2 tsp salt
- 4-6 small pieces of cooked shrimp, chicken, or mushrooms (optional)
- 2-3 thin slices of ginkgo nuts (optional)
- Chopped green onions for garnish

Instructions:

1. In a bowl, whisk the eggs. Add the dashi stock, soy sauce, mirin, and salt, and whisk gently until smooth.
2. Pour the mixture through a fine mesh strainer to remove any air bubbles or impurities.
3. Prepare small heatproof cups or bowls and place the optional fillings (shrimp, chicken, mushrooms, or ginkgo nuts) at the bottom.
4. Pour the egg mixture over the fillings.
5. Cover the bowls with a lid or foil. Steam over medium heat for 15-20 minutes, or until the custard is set but still smooth.
6. Garnish with chopped green onions and serve hot.

Daifuku (Sweet Mochi)

Ingredients:

- 1 cup glutinous rice flour (mochi flour)
- 1/4 cup sugar
- 1/2 cup water
- Cornstarch or potato starch for dusting
- 1/2 cup red bean paste (anko), or any filling of your choice (like strawberry)

Instructions:

1. In a microwave-safe bowl, mix the glutinous rice flour, sugar, and water.
2. Microwave on high for 1 minute. Stir the mixture, then microwave for another minute. Stir again, then microwave for 30 seconds until the mixture becomes a sticky dough.
3. Dust a clean surface with cornstarch. Place the mochi dough on it and let it cool slightly.
4. Divide the dough into 8-10 small portions. Flatten each piece into a circle.
5. Place a spoonful of red bean paste or your filling in the center and fold the dough around it, pinching the edges to seal.
6. Dust the finished daifuku with cornstarch to prevent sticking. Let them cool completely before serving.

Rice with Pickled Plums (Umeboshi)

Ingredients:

- 2 cups cooked Japanese short-grain rice
- 2-3 umeboshi (pickled plums)
- A small amount of pickled plum juice or a sprinkle of sesame seeds (optional)

Instructions:

1. Place the cooked rice in a bowl.
2. Gently remove the pit from the umeboshi and break the plum into small pieces, or place it whole on top of the rice.
3. Add a little of the pickled plum juice if desired.
4. Serve with a sprinkle of sesame seeds if desired. Enjoy as a simple side dish or meal.

Agedashi Tofu

Ingredients:

- 1 block firm tofu, cut into cubes
- 1/4 cup cornstarch or potato starch
- Oil for frying
- 1/4 cup dashi stock
- 2 tbsp soy sauce
- 1 tbsp mirin
- 1/2 tsp sugar
- Chopped green onions for garnish
- Grated daikon radish (optional)

Instructions:

1. Pat the tofu cubes dry with paper towels to remove excess moisture.
2. Coat the tofu cubes evenly with cornstarch.
3. Heat oil in a pan over medium heat and fry the tofu cubes until golden brown on all sides, about 4-5 minutes. Remove and drain on paper towels.
4. In a separate saucepan, combine dashi, soy sauce, mirin, and sugar. Bring it to a simmer, then remove from heat.
5. Serve the tofu cubes in a bowl and pour the hot dashi sauce over them. Garnish with green onions and grated daikon if desired.

Japanese Toast with Butter and Soy Sauce

Ingredients:

- 2 slices shoku pan (Japanese white bread)
- 1 tbsp unsalted butter
- 1 tbsp soy sauce

Instructions:

1. Toast the bread slices until golden brown.
2. Spread butter evenly on both slices of toast.
3. Drizzle soy sauce over the buttered toast and serve immediately.

Bento Box Breakfast

Ingredients:

- 1 egg (for tamagoyaki or hard-boiled egg)
- 1/2 cup rice (steamed or flavored)
- Pickles (such as umeboshi or pickled vegetables)
- Fresh fruit (such as orange slices or grapes)
- Small portions of protein (grilled salmon, sausage, or chicken)

Instructions:

1. Prepare the tamagoyaki (Japanese rolled omelette) or hard-boil the egg.
2. Cook and portion the rice.
3. Arrange the rice, egg, protein, pickles, and fruit neatly in a bento box.
4. Pack the bento and serve for breakfast or lunch.

Tofu Salad

Ingredients:

- 1 block firm tofu, drained and cubed
- 1 cucumber, thinly sliced
- 1 carrot, julienned
- 1/2 cup cherry tomatoes, halved
- 1 tbsp sesame oil
- 2 tbsp soy sauce
- 1 tsp rice vinegar
- 1 tsp honey or sugar (optional)
- Sesame seeds for garnish

Instructions:

1. In a bowl, mix the tofu, cucumber, carrot, and tomatoes.
2. In a small bowl, whisk together the sesame oil, soy sauce, rice vinegar, and honey (if using).
3. Pour the dressing over the salad and toss gently to combine.
4. Garnish with sesame seeds and serve chilled.

Shoku Pan (Japanese White Bread)

Ingredients:

- 3 cups bread flour
- 1 tbsp sugar
- 1 tbsp active dry yeast
- 1 cup warm milk
- 1/4 cup unsalted butter, softened
- 1 tsp salt
- 1 egg (optional, for brushing the top)

Instructions:

1. In a bowl, combine the warm milk, sugar, and yeast. Let it sit for 5 minutes until frothy.
2. Add the bread flour, salt, and softened butter to the yeast mixture. Knead the dough for 8-10 minutes until smooth and elastic.
3. Place the dough in a greased bowl, cover, and let it rise for 1-1.5 hours, or until doubled in size.
4. Punch down the dough and shape it into a loaf. Place the dough in a greased loaf pan.
5. Let the dough rise for another 30-40 minutes.
6. Preheat the oven to 350°F (175°C). If desired, brush the top with an egg wash.
7. Bake for 25-30 minutes, or until golden brown. Let it cool before slicing.

Udon Noodle Soup

Ingredients:

- 4 cups dashi stock
- 2 tbsp soy sauce
- 1 tbsp mirin
- 1 tbsp sake
- 1 tbsp sugar
- 1/2 lb udon noodles (fresh or frozen)
- 2 green onions, chopped
- 1 soft-boiled egg (optional)
- Toppings like tempura, kamaboko (fish cake), or nori (seaweed)

Instructions:

1. In a pot, combine dashi stock, soy sauce, mirin, sake, and sugar. Bring to a simmer over medium heat.
2. While the broth simmers, cook the udon noodles according to package instructions, then drain and set aside.
3. Once the broth is heated through, pour it into bowls.
4. Add the cooked udon noodles to the broth.
5. Top with chopped green onions, a soft-boiled egg, and any additional toppings like tempura or kamaboko.
6. Serve hot.

Japanese-style French Toast

Ingredients:

- 2 slices of shoku pan (Japanese white bread)
- 2 eggs
- 1/4 cup milk
- 1 tbsp sugar
- 1 tsp vanilla extract
- 1 tbsp butter
- Maple syrup or powdered sugar for serving

Instructions:

1. In a bowl, whisk together the eggs, milk, sugar, and vanilla extract.
2. Heat a skillet over medium heat and melt the butter.
3. Dip the bread slices into the egg mixture, making sure they are fully soaked.
4. Cook the bread slices in the skillet for 2-3 minutes on each side, until golden brown.
5. Serve with maple syrup or powdered sugar.

Mochi with Red Bean Paste

Ingredients:

- 1 cup glutinous rice flour (mochi flour)
- 1/4 cup sugar
- 1/2 cup water
- Cornstarch or potato starch for dusting
- 1/2 cup red bean paste (anko)

Instructions:

1. In a microwave-safe bowl, mix the glutinous rice flour, sugar, and water.
2. Microwave on high for 1 minute. Stir the mixture, then microwave for another minute. Stir again, then microwave for 30 seconds until the mixture becomes a sticky dough.
3. Dust a clean surface with cornstarch. Place the mochi dough on it and let it cool slightly.
4. Divide the dough into 8-10 small portions. Flatten each piece into a circle.
5. Place a spoonful of red bean paste in the center and fold the dough around it, pinching the edges to seal.
6. Dust the finished mochi with cornstarch to prevent sticking. Let them cool completely before serving.

Japanese Hot Dog Buns

Ingredients:

- 2 cups bread flour
- 1 tbsp sugar
- 1 tbsp active dry yeast
- 1/2 cup warm milk
- 1/4 cup water
- 2 tbsp unsalted butter, softened
- 1/2 tsp salt
- Hot dog sausages or franks (enough for the buns)
- Ketchup or mustard (optional)

Instructions:

1. In a small bowl, combine the warm milk, water, sugar, and yeast. Let it sit for 5 minutes until frothy.
2. In a large bowl, combine the bread flour and salt. Add the yeast mixture and softened butter.
3. Knead the dough for 8-10 minutes until smooth and elastic.
4. Cover the dough and let it rise in a warm place for 1 hour, or until doubled in size.
5. Punch down the dough and divide it into small pieces. Roll each piece into an oblong shape that fits the length of the hot dog sausage.
6. Place the buns on a baking sheet and let them rise for another 30-40 minutes.
7. Preheat the oven to 350°F (175°C) and bake for 15-20 minutes until golden brown.
8. Cool the buns and insert the hot dog sausages. Optionally, add ketchup or mustard before serving.

Rice with Pickled Vegetables

Ingredients:

- 2 cups cooked Japanese short-grain rice
- 1/4 cup pickled daikon radish, sliced
- 1/4 cup pickled cucumber, sliced
- 2 tbsp pickled ginger (optional)
- 1/4 cup umeboshi (pickled plums)

Instructions:

1. Place the cooked rice in a bowl.
2. Top with sliced pickled daikon, cucumber, and umeboshi.
3. Garnish with pickled ginger if desired. Serve as a side dish with other Japanese meals.

Japanese Scrambled Eggs

Ingredients:

- 2 eggs
- 1 tbsp soy sauce
- 1 tsp mirin
- 1 tbsp butter
- 1/2 tsp sugar (optional)
- Chopped green onions for garnish (optional)

Instructions:

1. In a bowl, whisk together the eggs, soy sauce, mirin, and sugar (if using).
2. Heat a non-stick skillet over low heat and melt the butter.
3. Pour the egg mixture into the skillet. Gently stir with chopsticks or a spatula in a circular motion.
4. Cook until the eggs are just set, but still soft and fluffy.
5. Garnish with chopped green onions and serve immediately.

Shrimp Tempura

Ingredients:

- 10 large shrimp, peeled and deveined
- 1/2 cup all-purpose flour
- 1/4 cup cornstarch
- 1/4 tsp baking powder
- 1/2 cup cold sparkling water
- Vegetable oil for frying
- Tempura dipping sauce

Instructions:

1. In a bowl, mix the flour, cornstarch, and baking powder. Gradually add the sparkling water, stirring gently to make a light batter.
2. Heat vegetable oil in a pot to 350°F (175°C).
3. Dip the shrimp into the batter, then carefully place them in the hot oil. Fry for 2-3 minutes until golden and crispy.
4. Remove the shrimp and drain on paper towels. Serve with tempura dipping sauce.

Miso-Marinated Fish

Ingredients:

- 2 pieces white fish fillets (such as cod or halibut)
- 2 tbsp white miso paste
- 1 tbsp mirin
- 1 tbsp sake
- 1 tbsp soy sauce
- 1 tsp sugar

Instructions:

1. In a bowl, combine miso paste, mirin, sake, soy sauce, and sugar to make the marinade.
2. Coat the fish fillets with the marinade and let them sit in the fridge for at least 30 minutes.
3. Preheat the grill or broiler to medium-high heat.
4. Grill or broil the fish for about 5-7 minutes on each side until cooked through.
5. Serve with rice and vegetables.

Katsuobushi (Dried Bonito Flakes) on Rice

Ingredients:

- 2 cups cooked Japanese short-grain rice
- 1/4 cup katsuobushi (dried bonito flakes)
- Soy sauce for drizzling

Instructions:

1. Place the cooked rice in a bowl.
2. Sprinkle the katsuobushi on top of the rice.
3. Drizzle with a small amount of soy sauce and serve.

Saba (Mackerel) with Rice

Ingredients:

- 2 saba (mackerel) fillets
- 2 tbsp soy sauce
- 1 tbsp mirin
- 1 tsp sake
- 2 cups cooked Japanese short-grain rice

Instructions:

1. In a small saucepan, combine soy sauce, mirin, and sake. Heat gently until the sauce thickens slightly.
2. Grill or pan-fry the mackerel fillets for 3-4 minutes on each side until cooked through.
3. Serve the mackerel fillets on top of the rice, drizzled with the sauce.

Japanese Milk Bread (Hokkaido Milk Bread)

Ingredients:

- 3 cups bread flour
- 2 tbsp sugar
- 1 tbsp active dry yeast
- 1/2 cup whole milk
- 1/4 cup heavy cream
- 1/4 cup warm water
- 1 tsp salt
- 1/4 cup unsalted butter, softened

Instructions:

1. In a small bowl, combine the warm water, sugar, and yeast. Let it sit for 5 minutes until frothy.
2. In a large bowl, combine the bread flour and salt. Add the yeast mixture, milk, and heavy cream.
3. Knead the dough for 8-10 minutes, then add the softened butter and continue kneading until smooth.
4. Cover the dough and let it rise for 1 hour, or until doubled in size.
5. Punch down the dough and divide it into three equal portions. Shape the portions into rolls and place them in a greased loaf pan.
6. Let the dough rise again for 30-40 minutes.
7. Preheat the oven to 350°F (175°C). Bake for 25-30 minutes until golden brown.
8. Let the bread cool before slicing.

Yuba (Tofu Skin) with Soy Sauce

Ingredients:

- 1 sheet of fresh yuba (tofu skin)
- 2 tbsp soy sauce
- 1 tbsp mirin
- 1 tsp sesame oil
- 1 tsp sugar
- 1 tbsp green onions, chopped (optional)

Instructions:

1. If using fresh yuba, cut it into strips or desired shape.
2. In a small saucepan, combine soy sauce, mirin, sesame oil, and sugar. Heat over medium heat until the sugar dissolves.
3. In a separate pan, quickly sear the yuba strips over medium heat until lightly crispy on both sides.
4. Drizzle the soy sauce mixture over the yuba and serve hot, garnished with chopped green onions if desired.

Sweet Red Bean Soup

Ingredients:

- 1 1/2 cups adzuki beans
- 5 cups water
- 1/2 cup sugar
- 1/4 tsp salt

Instructions:

1. Rinse the adzuki beans and place them in a pot with water. Bring to a boil, then reduce the heat and simmer for 1-2 hours, until the beans are soft.
2. Once the beans are cooked, add sugar and salt. Stir well until the sugar dissolves.
3. Serve the soup warm, optionally with mochi pieces or a drizzle of honey for added sweetness.

Ramen Soup with Boiled Egg

Ingredients:

- 2 cups chicken broth
- 2 cups water
- 2 tbsp soy sauce
- 1 tbsp miso paste (optional)
- 1 tbsp sesame oil
- 2 packs ramen noodles
- 2 soft-boiled eggs (peeled)
- 1/4 cup sliced green onions
- 1 sheet nori (seaweed)
- Toppings like sliced pork or bamboo shoots (optional)

Instructions:

1. In a pot, combine the chicken broth, water, soy sauce, miso paste, and sesame oil. Bring to a simmer.
2. Cook the ramen noodles according to the package instructions, then drain.
3. Place the cooked noodles in bowls and pour the hot broth over them.
4. Halve the soft-boiled eggs and place them on top of the ramen.
5. Garnish with sliced green onions, nori, and any additional toppings of your choice.
6. Serve hot.

Ebi Fry (Shrimp Fried Cutlet)

Ingredients:

- 10 large shrimp, peeled and deveined
- 1/2 cup flour
- 1 egg, beaten
- 1 cup panko breadcrumbs
- Vegetable oil for frying
- Tonkatsu sauce for dipping

Instructions:

1. Dip each shrimp in flour, then in the beaten egg, and coat it with panko breadcrumbs.
2. Heat vegetable oil in a deep pan to 350°F (175°C).
3. Fry the shrimp in batches for about 2-3 minutes until golden and crispy.
4. Remove the shrimp and drain on paper towels. Serve with tonkatsu sauce for dipping.

Matcha Green Tea Pancakes

Ingredients:

- 1 cup all-purpose flour
- 1 tbsp matcha powder
- 2 tbsp sugar
- 1 tsp baking powder
- 1/2 tsp baking soda
- 1/2 cup milk
- 1 egg
- 2 tbsp melted butter
- 1/2 tsp vanilla extract

Instructions:

1. In a bowl, whisk together the flour, matcha powder, sugar, baking powder, and baking soda.
2. In a separate bowl, whisk together the milk, egg, melted butter, and vanilla extract.
3. Pour the wet ingredients into the dry ingredients and stir until just combined.
4. Heat a non-stick skillet over medium heat and lightly grease with butter.
5. Pour 1/4 cup of batter onto the skillet for each pancake. Cook for 2-3 minutes on each side, until golden brown.
6. Serve with syrup or whipped cream.

Japanese Steamed Buns (Nikuman)

Ingredients:

- 2 cups all-purpose flour
- 2 tbsp sugar
- 1 tsp active dry yeast
- 1/2 cup warm water
- 1 tbsp vegetable oil
- 1/4 tsp salt
- Filling: 1/2 lb ground pork, 2 tbsp soy sauce, 1 tbsp sugar, 1 tbsp ginger (grated), 1 tbsp green onions (chopped)

Instructions:

1. In a bowl, mix the flour, sugar, and yeast. Gradually add warm water and knead until smooth. Let the dough rise for about 1 hour.
2. Meanwhile, mix together the ground pork, soy sauce, sugar, ginger, and green onions for the filling.
3. Punch down the dough and divide it into 6 equal pieces. Flatten each piece into a small circle.
4. Place a spoonful of filling in the center of each dough circle and fold the edges to seal.
5. Steam the buns in a bamboo steamer or metal steamer for 15-20 minutes until cooked through. Serve warm.

Donburi Rice Bowls

Ingredients:

- 2 cups cooked Japanese short-grain rice
- 1/2 lb meat of choice (chicken, beef, or pork), thinly sliced
- 1 onion, sliced
- 2 tbsp soy sauce
- 2 tbsp mirin
- 1 tbsp sugar
- 1/4 cup dashi stock
- 1 egg (optional)
- Chopped green onions for garnish

Instructions:

1. In a pan, sauté the onion until softened. Add the sliced meat and cook until browned.
2. Add soy sauce, mirin, sugar, and dashi stock to the pan. Bring to a simmer.
3. If using, crack an egg into the pan and cook it gently.
4. Spoon the cooked rice into bowls and top with the meat and sauce. Garnish with chopped green onions.

Mochi Ice Cream

Ingredients:

- 1 cup mochiko (sweet rice flour)
- 1/4 cup sugar
- 1 cup water
- 1/2 cup ice cream (flavor of your choice)

Instructions:

1. In a microwave-safe bowl, mix the mochiko, sugar, and water. Microwave for 1 minute, then stir. Repeat until the mixture thickens, about 2-3 minutes.
2. Dust a clean surface with cornstarch. Spread the mochi dough onto the surface and let it cool.
3. Once cooled, divide the mochi into small pieces. Flatten each piece and place a small scoop of ice cream in the center.
4. Carefully wrap the mochi around the ice cream and seal. Freeze until firm. Serve cold.

Tofu and Vegetable Stir-Fry

Ingredients:

- 1 block firm tofu, drained and cubed
- 1 tbsp soy sauce
- 1 tbsp sesame oil
- 1 tbsp rice vinegar
- 1/2 cup sliced bell peppers
- 1/2 cup sliced zucchini
- 1/4 cup sliced carrots
- 1/4 cup chopped green onions

Instructions:

1. Heat the sesame oil in a pan over medium heat. Add the tofu and cook until crispy and golden.
2. Add the vegetables to the pan and stir-fry for 3-4 minutes until tender.
3. Add soy sauce and rice vinegar, stir well, and cook for another 2 minutes.
4. Garnish with chopped green onions and serve hot.

Kake Gohan (Plain Rice with Toppings)

Ingredients:

- 2 cups cooked Japanese short-grain rice
- Toppings:
    - 1/4 cup pickled plum (umeboshi)
    - 1 sheet nori (seaweed)
    - 1 tsp sesame seeds
    - Soy sauce

Instructions:

1. Place the cooked rice in bowls.
2. Top with your choice of toppings, such as pickled plum, nori, and sesame seeds.
3. Drizzle with a little soy sauce and serve as a simple, comforting dish.

Tofu and Daikon Salad

Ingredients:

- 1/2 block firm tofu, cubed
- 1/2 daikon radish, peeled and julienned
- 1 cucumber, thinly sliced
- 1 tbsp rice vinegar
- 1 tbsp soy sauce
- 1 tsp sesame oil
- 1 tsp sugar
- 1 tbsp sesame seeds
- 1 tbsp chopped green onions

Instructions:

1. In a bowl, combine the tofu, daikon radish, and cucumber.
2. In a small bowl, whisk together rice vinegar, soy sauce, sesame oil, and sugar.
3. Pour the dressing over the tofu and vegetable mixture, tossing gently to combine.
4. Garnish with sesame seeds and chopped green onions.
5. Serve chilled as a refreshing side dish.

Oyakodon (Chicken and Egg Rice Bowl)

Ingredients:

- 2 chicken thighs, boneless and skinless, cut into bite-sized pieces
- 1 onion, thinly sliced
- 1/2 cup dashi stock
- 2 tbsp soy sauce
- 1 tbsp mirin
- 1 tbsp sugar
- 2 large eggs, beaten
- 2 cups cooked Japanese short-grain rice
- Chopped green onions for garnish

Instructions:

1. In a pan, sauté the chicken pieces and onions until the chicken is fully cooked.
2. Add dashi stock, soy sauce, mirin, and sugar to the pan. Bring to a simmer.
3. Once the liquid simmers, pour the beaten eggs over the chicken mixture. Cover the pan and cook for 2-3 minutes until the eggs are just set.
4. Serve the chicken and egg mixture over bowls of rice.
5. Garnish with chopped green onions and serve hot.

Okara (Soy Pulp) Patties

Ingredients:

- 1 cup okara (soy pulp)
- 1/4 cup panko breadcrumbs
- 1 egg, beaten
- 1/4 cup finely chopped green onions
- 1 tbsp soy sauce
- 1 tbsp mirin
- 1/4 tsp salt
- 1/4 tsp pepper
- Vegetable oil for frying

Instructions:

1. In a bowl, combine okara, panko breadcrumbs, egg, green onions, soy sauce, mirin, salt, and pepper. Mix until well combined.
2. Shape the mixture into small patties.
3. Heat vegetable oil in a pan over medium heat. Fry the patties for 2-3 minutes on each side, until golden brown.
4. Drain the patties on paper towels. Serve hot as a side dish or snack.

Japanese-style Oatmeal

Ingredients:

- 1 cup rolled oats
- 2 cups water
- 1/4 tsp salt
- 1 tbsp soy sauce
- 1 tbsp sesame oil
- 1/2 tsp pickled plum (umeboshi), chopped (optional)
- Chopped green onions for garnish

Instructions:

1. In a pot, bring the water to a boil and add the oats.
2. Reduce the heat and simmer for 5-7 minutes, stirring occasionally, until the oats are soft and the water is absorbed.
3. Stir in the salt, soy sauce, and sesame oil.
4. Serve hot, garnished with pickled plum (optional) and green onions.

Yakimeshi (Japanese Fried Rice)

Ingredients:

- 2 cups cooked Japanese short-grain rice (preferably cold)
- 1/2 cup diced chicken, shrimp, or vegetables
- 1/4 cup diced onion
- 1/4 cup diced carrots
- 1/4 cup peas
- 2 tbsp soy sauce
- 1 tbsp sesame oil
- 2 eggs, scrambled
- 2 tbsp chopped green onions

Instructions:

1. Heat sesame oil in a pan over medium heat. Add the onion, carrots, peas, and meat or vegetables. Cook until tender.
2. Add the cold rice and stir-fry, breaking up any clumps.
3. Stir in soy sauce and cook until the rice is well coated.
4. Push the rice to one side and scramble the eggs in the empty space. Once scrambled, mix the eggs into the rice.
5. Garnish with chopped green onions and serve hot.

Japanese Hot Pot (Shabu-Shabu)

Ingredients:

- 1/2 lb thinly sliced beef or pork
- 4 cups dashi broth
- 1 tbsp soy sauce
- 1 tbsp mirin
- 1/2 cup sliced mushrooms (shiitake or enoki)
- 1/2 cup sliced napa cabbage
- 1/2 cup sliced tofu
- 1/2 cup green onions, chopped
- Dipping sauce (ponzu sauce or sesame sauce)

Instructions:

1. Bring the dashi broth to a simmer in a large pot. Add soy sauce and mirin.
2. Add the cabbage, mushrooms, and tofu to the broth and cook for a few minutes until softened.
3. Dip the thinly sliced meat into the hot broth, cooking it briefly (about 30 seconds to 1 minute).
4. Serve the meat, vegetables, and tofu with dipping sauces.

Edamame and Rice

Ingredients:

- 2 cups cooked Japanese short-grain rice
- 1 cup edamame (young soybeans), boiled and salted
- 1 tbsp soy sauce
- 1 tbsp sesame oil
- 1 tbsp sesame seeds

Instructions:

1. In a bowl, mix the cooked rice, boiled edamame, soy sauce, and sesame oil.
2. Garnish with sesame seeds and serve warm.

Takoyaki (Octopus Balls)

Ingredients:

- 1 cup takoyaki flour (or all-purpose flour)
- 1 egg
- 1 1/4 cups dashi stock
- 1/2 cup chopped cooked octopus
- 1/4 cup chopped green onions
- 1/4 cup pickled ginger, chopped
- Takoyaki sauce (or okonomiyaki sauce)
- Bonito flakes
- Aonori (seaweed flakes)

Instructions:

1. Preheat a takoyaki pan over medium heat and lightly grease each mold.
2. Mix the takoyaki flour, egg, and dashi stock to create a batter.
3. Pour the batter into each mold, filling it halfway.
4. Add a piece of octopus, green onions, and pickled ginger to each mold.
5. Fill the molds with more batter, then cook for 3-4 minutes, turning the balls with chopsticks until golden and crispy.
6. Drizzle with takoyaki sauce, and garnish with bonito flakes and aonori. Serve hot.

Japanese Coffee Jelly

Ingredients:

- 2 cups brewed strong coffee
- 1/2 cup sugar
- 1 tsp agar-agar powder (or gelatin)
- Whipped cream for topping (optional)

Instructions:

1. In a saucepan, heat the coffee and sugar over medium heat until the sugar dissolves.
2. Sprinkle in the agar-agar powder (or dissolve gelatin in a little cold water if using) and bring to a boil, stirring constantly.
3. Pour the mixture into a mold and let it cool to room temperature. Then, refrigerate for at least 2 hours until set.
4. Once set, cut the coffee jelly into cubes and serve with whipped cream on top (optional).

www.ingramcontent.com/pod-product-compliance
Lightning Source LLC
LaVergne TN
LVHW081332060526
838201LV00055B/2595